People in the Community

Vets

Diyan Leake

Heinemann Library
Chicago, Illinois

Customer Service 888-454-2279
Visit our website at www.heinemannraintree.com

Designed by Joanna Hinton-Malivoire and Steve Mead
Printed in China by South China Printing Company Limited

12 11 10 09 08
10 9 8 7 6 5 4 3 2 1

Library of Congress Cataloguing-in-Publication Data
Leake, Diyan.
    Vets / Diyan Leake.
       p. cm. -- (People in the community)
    Includes bibliographical references and index.
    ISBN-13: 978-1-4329-1192-8 (hc)
    ISBN-13: 978-1-4329-1199-7 (pb)
    1. Veterinarians--Juvenile literature. 2. Veterinary medicine--Vocational guidance--Juvenile literature. I. Title.
    SF456.L43 2008
    636.089--dc22
                                  2007045069

Acknowledgments
The publishers would like to thank the following for permission to reproduce photographs:
©Alamy pp. **13** (Jim Wileman), **14** (Arco Images), **21** (Blend Images); ©Associated Press pp. **6** (Jessie Cohen), **10**, **17** (Steve Chernek), **22 (bottom)** (Steve Cherneck); ©Corbis pp. **15** (Larry Williams/Zefa), **19** (Jim Craigmyle), **20** (Frank Lukasseck); ©digitalrailroad (Stewart Cohen) pp. **8**, **22 (middle)**; ©Getty Images pp. **4** (Ingolf Pompe), **7** (Gary Benson), **9** (Li Zhong/ChinaFotoPress), **18** (Hassan Ammar/AFP), **22 (top)** (Ingolf Pompe); ©Peter Arnold Inc. pp. **11** (PHONE Labat J.M./Rouquette F.), **12** (PHONE Labat J.M./Rouquette F.), **16** (Jorgen Schytte); ©Shutterstock (Emin Kuliyev) p. **5**.

Front cover photograph of a vet examining a chimpanzee on Ngamba Island reproduced with permission of ©Corbis (Penny Tweedie). Back cover photograph reproduced with permission of ©Alamy (Blend Images).

Every effort has been made to contact copyright holders of any material reproduced in this book. Any omissions will be rectified in subsequent printings if notice is given to the publisher.

Contents

Communities

People live in communities.

People work in communities.

Vets in the Community

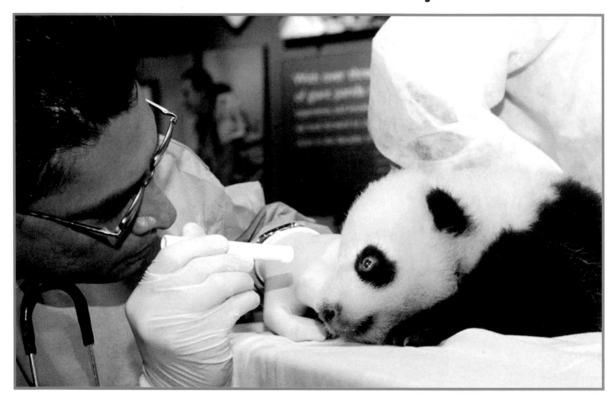

Vets work in communities.

Vets help animals stay healthy.

What Vets Do

Vets work with pets.

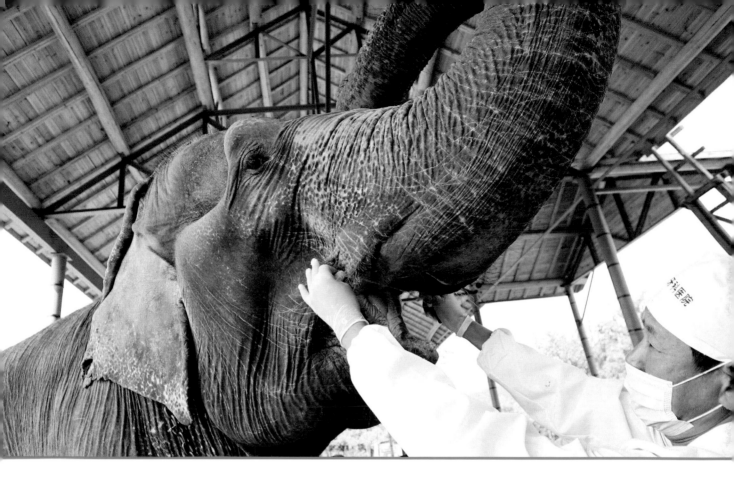

Vets work with wild animals.

Vets help animals when they are sick.

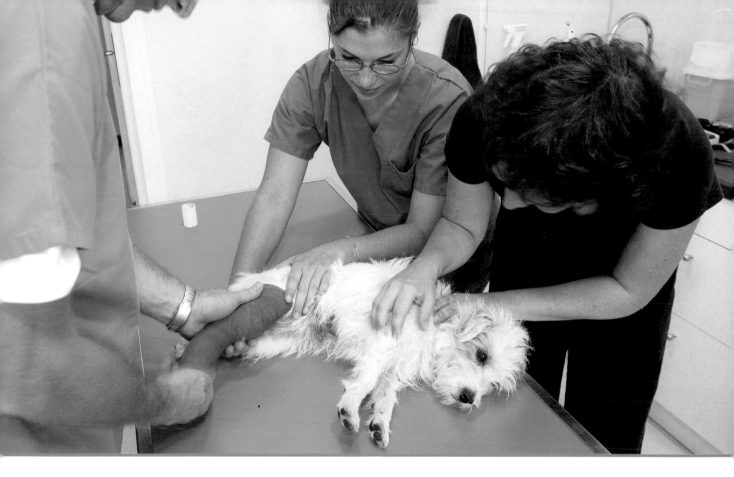

Vets help animals when they are hurt.

Where Vets Work

Vets work in offices.

Vets work at farms.

What Vets Use

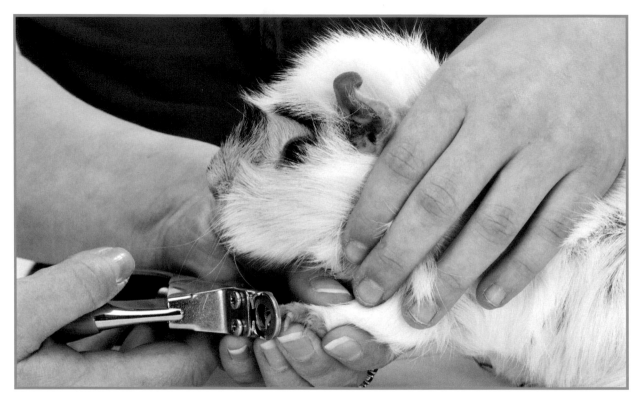

Vets use tools.

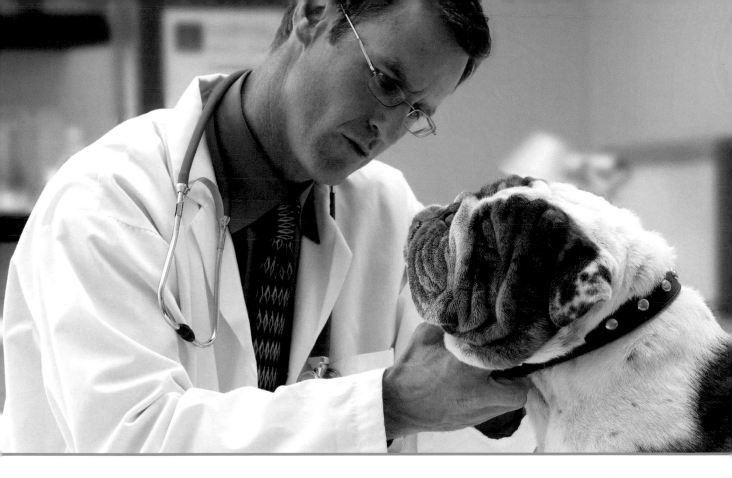

Vets use their hands.

People Who Work with Vets

Vets work with farmers.

Vets work with zookeepers.

Vets work with adults.

Vets work with children.

How Vets Help Us

Vets help animals stay healthy.

Vets help the community.

Picture Glossary

community group of people living and working in the same area

pet animal that lives with people in their home

zookeeper person who works with wild animals in a zoo

Index

Note to Parents and Teachers

This series introduces readers to the lives of different community workers, and explains some of the different jobs they perform around the world. Some of the locations featured include Zurich, Switzerland (page 4); New York City, NY (page 5); Washington, D.C. (page 6); Hangzhou, China (page 9); Ain Arab, Lebanon (page 18), and Ngamba Island (cover).

Discuss with children their experiences with vets in the community. Do they know any vets? Have they ever visited a veterinary clinic? What was it like? Discuss with children why communities need vets.

Ask children to look through the book and name some of the tools vets use to help them with their job. Give children poster boards and ask them to draw vets. Tell them to show the clothes, tools, and vehicles they use to do their job.

The text has been chosen with the advice of a literacy expert to enable beginning readers success while reading independently or with moderate support. You can support children's nonfiction literacy skills by helping them use the table of contents, picture glossary, and index.